Lion Christmas Favourites
for the very young

LION
CHILDREN'S

Contents

I count the days to Christmas

by Lois Rock

illustrated by Sheila Moxley

I count the days to Christmas
and I watch the evening sky.
I want to see the angels
as to Bethlehem they fly.

I'm watching for the wise men
and the royal shining star.
Please may I travel with them?
Is the stable very far?

I count the days to Christmas
as we shop and bake and clean.
The lights and tinsel sparkle,
and yet deep inside I dream

that as we tell the story
of Lord Jesus and his birth,
the things of every day will fade
as heaven comes to earth.

Mary and the Angel

by Mary Joslin
illustrated by Elena Temporin

One day, God sent the angel Gabriel to earth, to a little town named Nazareth. Its mud-brick houses stood on a hilltop above fields and orchards, and in the springtime of the year the warm breezes set the blossom trees fluttering.

Among them sat a young woman named Mary. She was enjoying the sunshine and dreaming of her wedding. All at once, Gabriel appeared. 'Peace be with you,' said the angel.

Mary jumped in alarm. 'Do not be afraid,' said Gabriel. 'God has chosen you to give birth to a son, and you will name him Jesus. He will be a king, and his kingdom will never end.'

'How can that be?' asked Mary. She sounded worried and yet disbelieving too. 'I'm a virgin, not yet married.'

'God will make all this come true,' replied the angel. 'For this reason, the holy child will be called the son of God.'

Mary gazed back. The angel, the blossom, the clouds in the sky… suddenly they all seemed to be part of heaven itself.

'I will do as God wants,' said Mary humbly. 'May everything happen as you have said.'

Gabriel bowed low – and vanished.

The First Christmas

by Sophie Piper
illustrated by Estelle Corke

Long ago, in the little town of Nazareth, there lived a girl named Mary.

She grew up believing in God. She grew up wanting to do the things that are right and good.

As she grew up, she looked forward to getting married. It was all arranged that she would marry Joseph.

One day, an angel came to her with a message.

'God has blessed you,' said the angel. 'You are going to have a baby boy: Jesus. He will do wonderful things. People will say he is the Son of God.'

Mary was puzzled. 'I'm not married yet,' she explained.

'God will make everything come true,' said the angel.

'I will be happy to do what God wants,' replied Mary.

Joseph was upset by Mary's news.

'Mary's baby isn't my baby,' he said. 'Perhaps I shouldn't marry her.'

That night, he had a dream. An angel spoke to him:

'Please look after Mary and her baby. Everything will be all right.'

Soon after, Joseph went to find Mary. 'I still want us to be husband and wife,' he said to her.

'Now, I know you've heard about the emperor – that he wants to have a new list of all the people in his empire.

'I want us to go to my home town of Bethlehem together. There we shall put our names on the list as a family.'

When they got to Bethlehem, there was a problem.

'No one has any spare room,' explained Joseph. 'We have to shelter in an animal shed.'

That night, Mary's baby, Jesus, was born. She wrapped him up snugly.

'This manger can be his cradle,' said Joseph.

On the hills nearby were some shepherds. They were looking after their sheep.

They were watching for danger. Who could tell what lurked in the shadows?

Suddenly, the sky was bright.

An angel appeared. 'I have good news. A baby has been born in Bethlehem. He will bring God's blessings to all the world. Go and find him. He's sleeping in a manger.'

Then more and more angels appeared, all singing to God.

All of a sudden, the angels disappeared. Everything was dark again.

'Let's go to Bethlehem,' said the shepherds.

They went and found Mary and Joseph and the baby.

Everything was just as the angel had said.

Not very far away was the city of Jerusalem. Some people had gone on a long journey to see the king there.

'We're following a star,' they said.

'It is shining because a new king has been born. Is he here?'

The king frowned and shook his head. 'There's an old story that the greatest king ever will be born in Bethlehem,' he said.

'I want you to go there. If you find a new king, be sure to tell me where he is.'

The men set out for Bethlehem.

'I hope this is the right way,' said one.

'Oh look!' said a second. 'There's our star again!'

'I'm glad we've come,' said a third. 'I think we've been very wise.'

The star shone down on a little house in Bethlehem. The wise men went inside. They saw Mary and her baby.

'This is the king we have been looking for!' they said.

They gave him gifts: gold, frankincense and myrrh.

That night, they dreamed the same dream. An angel told them not to go back to the king. They agreed to go home a different way.

Soon after, Joseph came hurrying to Mary and Jesus.

'I love you both so much,' he said. 'Now a dream has got me worried. I'm afraid we won't be safe here in Bethlehem. Let's leave at once.

The three of them journeyed on.

Mary held Jesus tight. After all that had happened, she felt sure of one thing:

Her little baby must truly be God's own Son, and she would keep him safe.

The Friendly Beasts

Anonymous
illustrated by Alex Ayliffe

Jesus our brother, kind and good,
Was humbly born in a stable rude,
And the friendly beasts around him stood;
Jesus our brother, kind and good.

'I,' said the donkey, shaggy and brown,
'I carried his mother up hill and down,
I carried her safely to Bethlehem town;
'I,' said the donkey, shaggy and brown.

'I,' said the cow, all white and red,
'I gave him my manger for his bed,
I gave him my hay to pillow his head;
'I,' said the cow, all white and red.

'I,' said the sheep, with the curly horn,
'I gave him my wool for his blanket warm;
He wore my coat on Christmas morn;
'I,' said the sheep, with the curly horn.

'I,' said the dove, from the rafters high,
'Cooed him to sleep, my mate and I;
We cooed him to sleep, my mate and I;
'I,' said the dove, from the rafters high.

And every beast, by some good spell,
In the stable dark, was glad to tell,
Of the gift he gave Emmanuel,
The gift he gave Emmanuel.

The Christmas Play

by Clare Bevan
Illustrated by Julie Park

Here is an inn with a stable,
Equipped with some straw and a chair.
Here is an angel in bed sheets,
With tinsel to tie back her hair.

Here is a servant in bathtowels,
Who sweeps round the stage with a broom.
Here is a chorus of faces,
All eager to cry out, 'NO ROOM!'

Here is a Joseph who stammers,
And tried to remember his lines.
Here is a teacher in anguish,
Who frantically gestures and signs.

Here is 'Away In A Manger' –
A tune MOST recorders can play.
Here is the moment of wonder,
As Jesus appears in the hay.

Here is a Mary with freckles,
Whose baby is plastic and hard.
Here is a donkey in trousers,
With ears made from pieces of card.

18

Here is a shepherd in curtains,
Who carries a crook made of wire.
Here is a boy sucking cough sweets,
Who growls from the back of the choir.

Here is a king bearing bath salts,
Who points at a star hung on strings.
Here is a dove who has stage-fright,
And quivers her crêpe-paper wings.

Here is a page boy in slippers,
Who stumbles his way up the stairs.
Here is a long line of cherubs,
Who march round the manger in pairs.

Here is a camel who fidgets,
With plasters stuck over his knee.
Here are some sheep who just giggle,
And think no one out there can see.

Here is a Herod in glasses,
Who whispers, so nobody hears.
Here is a Mum with a hanky,
To cover her pride and her tears.

Here is our final production,
And though it's still held up with pins,
The parents will love every minute –
For this is where Christmas begins.

May God Bless

by Lois Rock
Illustrated by Melanie Mitchell

Let us remember Mary this Christmas
And may God bless our mothers.

Let us remember Joseph this Christmas
And may God bless our fathers.

Let us remember the shepherds this Christmas
And may God bless all those who will be working.

Let us remember the wise men this Christmas
And may God bless all those who will be travelling.

Let us remember Jesus this Christmas
And may God bless us all and make us his children.

Ituku's Christmas Journey

by Elena Pasquali

Illustrated by Dubravka Kolanovic

Little Ituku sat outside his snow house. He always liked to watch when the magic lights streamed across the northern sky.

'I always think they are shining from heaven,' said Ituku to his faithful dog, Jaq. Jaq gave a little howl to show he agreed. As the two watched, the ribbons of light parted. A yellow shape uncurled in the sky and became a giant polar bear.

'Do not be afraid,' said the bear. Its voice was deep but gentle. 'I bring good news. The king of heaven has been born on earth. You must go and see him.'

Then it was all dark again. As soon as the sun rose, Ituku packed his kayak for a long journey. Jaq took his place on the front deck and together they set off across the icy sea.

Soon Ituku's kayak was being swept along, faster than he could ever have paddled. By evening, they had reached a land with snow-covered hills. They pulled the kayak up on the pebbly beach and found a sheltered hollow where they could sleep.

A snowshoe hare came out to look. Jaq wanted to bark with excitement – but he remembered to be polite and managed to swallow a tiny squeal instead.

'We are looking for the king of heaven,' explained Ituku. 'May we rest here one night?'

The hare nodded and scampered away. In the night, when Ituku and Jaq were fast asleep, the hare came back with all his friends. They snuggled around the boy and his dog to keep them warm.

The following day, Ituku and Jaq journeyed on, and in the evening the bright glow of a fire led them to another shore.

'I hope your dog knows how to behave,' said a gruff voice. 'We don't want him worrying our sheep.'

Jaq sat down obediently and Ituku spoke to the shepherds. 'We are looking for the king of heaven,' he said. "Is he here?'

The shepherds shook their heads. 'Not here,' they said. 'But there is a story about him. In a faraway land, the story says, angels told shepherds where to find the king of heaven. If it is true, you have a long way to go.'

The next day's paddling left Ituku feeling tired. He was resting his arms when a fishing boat came sailing along.

'Come aboard!' called the boy in the boat. 'Come to my home for the night. In my boat we can let the wind blow us to shore.'

As they flew through the sparkling water, Ituku told of his search.

'We are looking for the king of heaven,' he told the fisherboy.

'Really?' replied his companion. 'Where I come from, we tell stories of a king of heaven who will be a friend to fishermen. I hope you find him.'

After a wonderful meal in the fishing village and a good night's sleep, Ituku and Jaq were eager to journey on. The air was warmer in this region and the sea was calm.

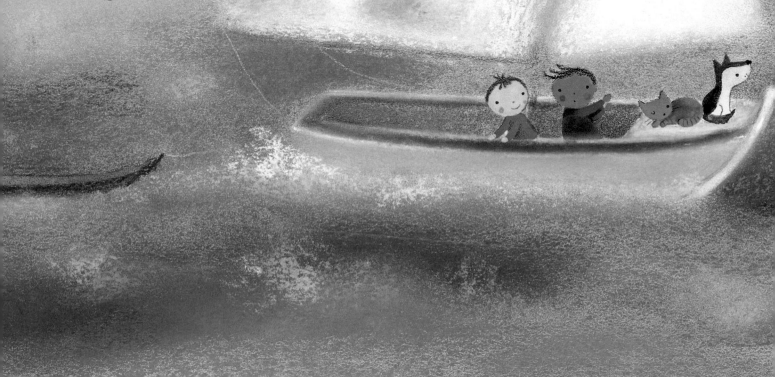

A land that was the colour of gold shimmered in the sun. They saw three travellers riding camels close to shore and wanted to ask them about the king, but by the time Ituku had found a place to land the travellers had gone too far in a different direction.

A desert fox came and sniffed at them.

'Don't you have a hole to go to?' it asked.

'We are on a journey,' replied Ituku. 'We are looking for the king of heaven.'

'Ah, that explains it,' said the fox. 'The king of heaven doesn't have a home either.' And off he went.

Ituku and Jaq huddled together to sleep. But in the cold desert night, mice squeaked and skittered and a long-eared owl hooted its haunting song. Ituku gave up trying to sleep. He watched the stars come out. Then he blinked: there was a new star… brighter and more beautiful than any other.

'Come, Jaq,' whispered Ituku. 'Let's paddle closer.'

They set out across the silverlit sea, but the star seemed to be drifting away ahead of them.

Then came the dawn, and Ituku wanted to rest. He paddled to shore, he could just feel the sand beneath his kayak when a pack of dogs came racing towards them. Behind them came soldiers brandishing weapons.

'You… you in the boat,' they shouted. 'Do you know anything about a newborn king?'

Ituku would have answered but Jaq was clearly scared. He barked and barked, and Ituku paddled away.

Ituku decided to spend the day fishing, letting the waves carry his kayak this way and that. When the hold was full of fish, he made his way to a sheltered cove.

There were people there. Smiling and waving.

'May I use your fire to cook my fish?' Ituku asked. 'We have plenty to share.'

'Of course,' said the man. 'I am Joseph, this is Mary and here is our new baby, Jesus.'

All at once Ituku knew he was looking at the newborn king of heaven. Jaq came and gave a joyful woof. The baby laughed.

Ituku shared the fish he had caught; the little family shared their bread and wine.

The next day, Joseph and Mary and Jesus travelled on.

Ituku and Jaq set out for home. 'Wherever we go,' said Ituku, 'we must tell people that the king of heaven has been born.'

'We will tell them that the best thing they can do is to make their own journey to find him.'

The First Christmas Tree

by John Goodwin
Illustrated by Richard Johnson

How will you decorate your Christmas tree this year? Will you use sparkling lights? This is the story of the first Christmas tree and is told by a fir tree deep in a forest.

It was a bitterly cold day and the ground was as hard as iron. I was shivering from the depths of my roots to the tips of my cones.

There was a sound far off on the edge of the wood.

'Listen,' called the holly tree in a prickly voice.

The noise sounded again, only this time it was louder and closer.

'It's coming this way,' said the sycamore.

'Footsteps. It's footsteps,' cried the chestnut.

Then we saw them. Two small figures, huddled close together for warmth, were walking slowly through the wood.

'Look,' said the larch. 'One of them is carrying a baby.'

'A baby so small,' whispered the willow.

'Too cold. Too cold,' hooted an owl high on a beech tree branch.

The couple came to a halt in our small glade. We could see that one was a man with a beard, and the other must have been the baby's mother, with a blue shawl. The baby looked so tiny and its clear eyes were wide open. The couple looked first this way and then that way, still they didn't move.

'They must be lost,' said the oak. 'They don't know which way to go.'

The mother reached out a hand to try and pull the blanket a little tighter around the baby's body.

'The baby will freeze to death,' worried the wild cherry.

Just then a fleck of snow drifted down on the wind, followed by another and another. The sky grew greyer by the second.

'They're shivering,' said the sycamore. 'And soon it will be dark.'

The spindle tree tossed its slender head and shook its slender trunk. Its scarlet berries jangled.

'We must do something. Do something,' it cried.

'What can we do?' whispered the willow, weeping a little.

'If only we had legs,' said the larch, 'we could run to make a shelter for them. But all our roots are fixed in the earth.'

'All my leaves have fallen,' sighed the oak. 'I can't offer them any protection against the bitter cold.'

I looked at the baby again with my evergreen eyes. It was now or never. I reached out with my branches and gave them a shake. A few of my cones fell to the ground. The mother's head turned towards me and so did the tiny baby's with eyes wider than ever. Then they came to me and sheltered under my bushy branches. I let my branches lower slowly, slowly, round them and soon the baby was fast asleep.

'Well done, fir tree,' whispered the willow.

'Amazing,' announced the ash.

The sky grew darker and the snow came thicker, but they were safe now.

'Perfect bliss,' I said to myself, and a little tear fell from my eye. Soon the tears were flowing freely and there was nothing I could so to stop them. But as they fell they didn't spill onto the sleeping travellers. Oh no.

As the tears trickled downwards they froze in long icicles all the way to the ground.

Early next morning, the sun came out and the icicles shone like bright jewels in the clear air. When the baby opened his eyes, my sparkling gems were the first thing he saw. The sparkle shone in his eyes too, and looking up at me, he smiled.

Christmas poems
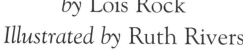

by Lois Rock
Illustrated by Ruth Rivers

I will choose a Christmas tree
to celebrate the Birth:
I will plant it carefully
upon God's good deep earth.

I will tend my Christmas tree
in honour of the Child:
I will leave it growing
in the wetness and the wild.

Christmas is expensive,
   my grandma said to me,
Except for Christmas starlight,
   which shines on earth for free,
And frost like silver tinsel
   on every woodland tree
And all the love that we can share together,
   you and me.

The Christmas lights are flashing
in gold and red and green
but, clear above, the starlight
is silver and serene.

Little Brigid

by Lois Rock ★ *Illustrated by* Alex Ayliffe

Little Brigid sat by the fire. She was mending her cloak.

'Oh dear,' she sighed. 'There seem to be holes everywhere. The cloth is old.

'Really, I should make a new cloak. Winter has only just begun. But I'm so busy every day.'

She was tired too. She rubbed her eyes and went to bed.

Brigid always got up early to do the daily jobs. First she mixed a bowl of bread and left it to rise. Then she went to call the cows for milking.

Then she came back to the kitchen. She baked the bread.

She made a pot of soup and left it cooking.

She churned some butter.

One winter's day, she heard a knock at the door.

Outside was a poor man. 'Can you spare something to eat?' he begged.

'Yes,' said Brigid. 'Come inside.'

She gave him warm soup and fresh bread spread with new butter.

Later, as she waved him goodbye, she saw a young woman with a crutch.

'Come and rest,' called Brigid. 'You must let your ankle get better.'

She took off the grubby bandage and washed the woman's feet.

She wrapped the hurt ankle in a new bandage.

'It feels better already,' said the woman.

That night, something woke Brigid – the sound of someone creeping in the door.

'Please help,' said a shy voice.

'You poor child,' said Brigid. 'You're wearing just a nightshirt.'

'Please come and rock the baby to sleep,' said the little child. 'His mother is so tired.

'Yes, of course,' said Brigid, wrapping her cloak around her. 'You show me the way.'

The little child seemed almost to fly along the woodland path. Brigid could hardly keep up.

All at once, they were there. Brigid found herself in a tumbledown room. At one end were a donkey and an ox. Nearer the door were a mother and her baby.

'Oh, he's only just been born!' said Brigid to the mother. ' Let me wrap him in my cloak. I will rock him to sleep and you can rest. Softly she sang a lullaby. The little child joined in the tune. He had the voice of an angel.

As the sun rose, the mother awoke. 'Bless you for coming to help,' she said.

Brigid hurried away. She felt warm and snug.

'My cloak!' she said. 'It's better than when it was new!' The cloak was thick and soft. The holes had gone. In their place were stars stitched in threads of gold.

The Baker's Christmas

by Christina Goodings
Illustrated by Liz Pichon

Ding, dong! Ding, dong!

It was Christmas night, and the church bells were calling the village folk to come together to hear again the story of the birth of Jesus at the start of their Christmas holiday.

'It's all very well for some people to stop work,' grumbled the baker, 'but people will still want their bread in the morning.'

He pulled on his boots and stamped off through the snow to the kitchen behind his shop.

He heaved open a great sack, and scooped flour into his bowl.

'I suppose I ought to make more than usual,' he thought moodily. 'I suppose people will be feasting.' So he put in extra flour.

He lifted the cover from a little bowl, and he took a spoonful of yeast.

He dipped his hand into a jar, and grasped a handful of salt.

Then he took a jug of water and poured it in to make his dough.

He stirred to the left and he stirred to the right.

He gathered the dough in his hands and squeezed it and pulled it, pushed it and pummelled it, squashed it and flattened it.

At last he had done the kneading. Wearily he wiped his hands.

Now I must shape the dough into loaves,' he said aloud, and he began to make all kinds of loaves: round loaves and long loaves, plain loaves and plaited loaves.

He filled three great trays with loaves and left them to rise while he built up the fire in the oven.

When he turned round, he could not believe what he saw. It seemed as if the loaves were moving. He rubbed his eyes. 'I must be very tired tonight,' he said. But when he looked again, he was even more baffled.

The loaves had changed shape. When there had been loaves, there were now tiny children: sitting, and stretching, standing and walking, running and dancing.

As the baker watched in amazement, the children danced right off the tray and across the floor. 'Come back, come back!' ordered the baker.

But the children took no notice. They just went on dancing and spinning right across the floor of his kitchen, through the door and out into the street.

'My bread, my customers,' cried the baker. 'Whatever will become of me if there is no bread in the morning?'

He ran after the dancing children as fast as he could.

They led him down the street, across the square, and up the little hill to the church. The little dough children ran inside, and the baker followed them.

There, in the corner, the village children had gathered around the little scene of the stable in Bethlehem. They were singing a carol, and their eyes were shining with wonder and delight at the sight of Mary and Joseph and the tiny baby. The clay figures were old and shabby, but even so, in the flickering candlelight, they shone with a light so clear and golden it could have been the light of heaven itself.

The dough children joined in the carol. None of the children appeared to notice, but it seemed to the baker that the song had never sounded so clear and tuneful.

As the last chorus echoed into silence, the dough children gathered together and tiptoed out of the church.

Out in the dark night, the baker could hardly see where they went, but he thought it was in the direction of his shop, so he hurried along as fast as he could.

When he got there, everything was calm. There were no dough children to be seen. The loaves on the trays had risen round and plump, just as they always did. The fire in the oven burnt with a cheerful orange glow. The room felt brighter and warmer and more welcoming than the baker could ever remember.

'How lucky I am to have this work to do!' exclaimed the baker. 'Here, in my kitchen, I too will celebrate Christmas.' While the loaves baked in the oven, he bought out flour and sugar, eggs and treacle, spices and raisins, and set to making sweet biscuits.

He chuckled as he rolled out the dough and cut it into fancy shapes.

'A treat for every child,' he said.

Winter Poems

Illustrated by Jan Lewis

There was an old person of Mold
Who shrank from sensations of cold;
So he purchased some muffs,
Some furs and some fluffs,
And wrapped himself from the cold.

Edward Lear

Frost white morning
Very Crisp-mas.

All the aunties
Scary Kiss-mas.

Fun and laughter
Merry Christmas!

Compiled by Lois Rock
This edition copyright © 2008 Lion Hudson
Text and illustrations copyright: see acknowledgments below

The moral rights of the authors and illustrators
have been asserted

A Lion Children's Book
an imprint of
Lion Hudson plc
Wilkinson House, Jordan Hill Road,
Oxford OX2 8DR, England
www.lionhudson.com
ISBN: 978-0-7459-6108-8

First edition 2008
10 9 8 7 6 5 4 3 2 1 0

A catalogue record for this book is available
from the British Library

Printed and bound in China

Acknowledgments

Cover (clockwise from top left): Melanie Mitchell (also, centre), Sheila Moxley, Dubravka Kolanovic, Richard Johnson, Liz Pichon, Mique Moriuchi. Copyright © individual illustrators listed above.
Endpages: 'It's Christmas time' by Lois Rock from *Celebrating Christmas* by Christina Goodings, copyright © 1998 Lion Hudson. 'The stars that shine at Christmas' by Lois Rock from *The Lion Book of 1000 Prayers for Children* by Lois Rock, copyright © 2003 Lion Hudson. Illustration from *Goodnight Prayers* by Sophie Piper, copyright © 2008 Mique Moriuchi.
I Count the Days to Christmas: Text first published in *My Very First Prayers*, copyright © 2003 Lion Hudson. Illustrations from *100 Favourite Prayers*. Illustrations copyright © 2006 Sheila Moxley.
Mary and the Angel: Text (adapted) and illustrations taken from *The Lion Treasury of Angel Stories* by Mary Joslin. Text copyright © 2006 Lion Hudson. Illustrations copyright © 2006 Elena Temporin.
The First Christmas: First published by Lion Hudson as a picture story book with this title in 2006. Text copyright © 2006 Lion Hudson. Illustrations copyright © 2006 Estelle Corke.
The Friendly Beasts: Illustration taken from *My Very First Bible* by Lois Rock, copyright © 2003 Alex Ayliffe.
The Christmas Play: Text first published in *Star of Wonder*, copyright © 1996 Claire Bevan. Illustrations taken from *The Christmas Play* by Claire Bevan, copyright © 1999 Julie Park.
May God Bless: Text adapted from 'A Christmas Blessing' from *The Lion Book of 1000 Prayers for Children* by Lois Rock, copyright © 2003 Lion Hudson. Illustrations from *The Christmas Story (See and Say!)* by Victoria Tebbs, copyright © 2006 Melanie Mitchell.

Ituku's Christmas Journey: Text adapted from the picture story book of the same title. Text copyright © 2005 Lion Hudson. Illustrations copyright © 2005 Dubravka Kolanovic.
The First Christmas Tree: Taken from *The Lion Book of Five-Minute Christmas Stories*. Text copyright © 2007 John Goodwin. Illustrations copyright © 2007 Richard Johnson.
Christmas Poems: 'I will choose a Christmas Tree' and 'The Christmas lights are flashing' taken from *The Lion Book of Christmas Poems* compiled by Sophie Piper, copyright © 2007 Lion Hudson. 'Christmas is expensive' taken from *What Will You Wear to Go Swimming?* by Lois Rock, copyright © 2002 Lion Hudson. Illustrations taken from *This Amazing World* by Lois Rock, copyright © 2002 Ruth Rivers.
Litle Brigid: Text and illustrations taken from *My Very First Christmas* by Lois Rock. Text copyright © 2006 Lion Hudson. Illustrations copyright © 2006 Alex Ayliffe.
The Baker's Christmas: Text and illustrations taken from *Celebrating Christmas* by Christina Goodings. Text copyright © 1998 Lion Hudson. Illustrations copyright © 1998 Liz Pichon.
Winter Poems: 'Frost white morning' taken from *The Lion Book of Christmas Poems* compiled by Sophie Piper, copyright © 2007 Lion Hudson. Illustration taken from *Around the Year* by Christina Goodings, copyright © 2001 Jan Lewis.